Ladybugs

by Cheryl Coughlan

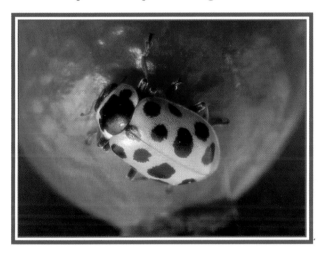

Consulting Editor: Gail Saunders-Smith, Ph.D.

Consultant: Gary A. Dunn, Director of Education,
Young Entomologists' Society

Pebble Books

an imprint of Capstone Press
Mankato, Minnesota

1

Pebble Books are published by Capstone Press
818 North Willow Street, Mankato, Minnesota 56001
http://www.capstone-press.com

Library of Congress Cataloging-in-Publication Data
Coughlan, Cheryl.
    Ladybugs/by Cheryl Coughlan.
        p. cm.—(Insects)
    Includes bibliographical references (p. 23) and index.
    Summary: Simple text and photographs introduce the physical features
of ladybugs.
        ISBN 0-7368-0242-8
        1. Ladybugs—Juvenile literature. [1. Ladybugs.] I. Title. II. Series: Insects
(Mankato, Minn.)
QL596.C65C68   1999
595.76′9—dc21   98-43878
                                                                                                      CIP
                                                                                                       AC

Note to Parents and Teachers

The Insects series supports national science standards for units on
the diversity and unity of life. The series shows that animals have
features that help them live in different environments. This book
describes and illustrates the parts of ladybugs. The photographs
support early readers in understanding the text. The repetition of
words and phrases helps early readers learn new words. This book
also introduces early readers to subject-specific vocabulary words,
which are defined in the Words to Know section. Early readers may
need assistance to read some words and to use the Table of
Contents, Words to Know, Read More, Internet Sites, and
Index/Word List sections of the book.

Table of Contents

4

Ladybugs are beetles.

Many ladybugs are
red or orange.

Many ladybugs have black spots.

Ladybugs have six legs.

hard wings

Ladybugs have
two hard wings.

soft wings

Ladybugs have
two soft wings.

head

Ladybugs have
a small head.

jaws

Ladybugs have strong jaws.

Most ladybugs eat
other insects.

Words to Know

beetle—an insect with one pair of hard wings and one pair of soft wings; the hard front wings are called elytra; ladybugs are sometimes called ladybird beetles.

insect—a small animal with a hard outer shell, three body parts, six legs, and two antennas; insects may have two or four wings.

jaw—a mouthpart used to grab things, bite, and chew; ladybugs use their powerful jaws to bite and eat aphids and other insects.

wing—a movable part of an insect that helps it fly; ladybugs have hard front wings that cover soft back wings; the hard wings are not used for flight.

Read More

Crewe, Sabrina. *The Ladybug.* Life Cycles. Austin, Texas: Raintree Steck-Vaughn, 1997.

Himmelman, John. *A Ladybug's Life.* Nature Upclose. New York: Children's Press, 1998.

Ross, Michael Elsohn. *Ladybugology.* Backyard Buddies. Minneapolis: Carolrhoda Books, 1997.

Wilsdon, Christina. *National Audobon Society First Field Guide: Insects.* New York: Scholastic, 1998.

Internet Sites

Buzzwords—A Glossary of Minibeast Terms
http://members.aol.com/YESedu/glossary.html

Ladybug
http://www.worldbook.com/fun/wbla/camp/html/walkldy.html

The Seven-Spot Ladybug
http://www.worldkids.net/critters/bugs/ladybug.htm

Index/Word List

Word Count: 42
Early-Intervention Level: 6

Editorial Credits

Martha E. Hillman, editor; Timothy Halldin, cover designer; Kimberly Danger, photo researcher

Photo Credits

Barrett & Mackay, 16
Bill Beatty, 6, 10
Dwight R. Kuhn, 18
James P. Rowan, 8
Photophile/Anthony Mercieca, 4, 14, 20
Robert McCaw, cover, 1
Root Resources/Anthony Mercieca, 12